Critical Praise for Pablo d'Ors

"The particular intensity of d'Ors' writing recalls the best of Bolaño."

—**PABLO M. ZARRACINA,**
EL CORREO ESPAÑOL

"There has been no greater innovation in Spanish fiction since Bolaño, nor a more original literary approach."

—**MIHÁLY DÉS,** *LATERAL*

"Pablo d'Ors is a sublime writer."

—**GABI MARTÍNEZ,** *QUÉ LEER*

"Pablo d'Ors is the most European of all Spanish writers—his works are ontologies."

—**DIEGO MEDRANO,** *EL COMERCIO*

"The books written by Pablo d'Ors are not like any other books.... His is a traveled and cosmopolitan literature."

—**ELOY TIZÓN, AUTHOR OF**
VELOCIDAD EN LOS JARDINES

BIOGRAPHY OF SILENCE

BIOGRAPHY OF SILENCE

AN ESSAY ON MEDITATION

PABLO d'ORS

TRANSLATED FROM
THE SPANISH
BY DAVID SHOOK

**PARALLAX
PRESS**

BERKELEY, CALIFORNIA

Parallax Press
P.O. Box 7355
Berkeley, California 94707
parallax.org

Parallax Press is the publishing division of Plum Village Community of Engaged
Buddhism, Inc.

Cover and text design by John Miller
Cover art ©Getty Images 737147111
Printed on 30% post-consumer waste recycled paper

Library of Congress Cataloging-in-Publication Data

Names: Ors, Pablo J. d', 1963- author.
Title: Biography of silence : an essay on meditation / Pablo d'Ors.
Other titles: Biografia del silencio. English
Description: Berkeley : Parallax Press, 2018.
Identifiers: LCCN 2018010891 (print) | LCCN 2018034949 (ebook) | ISBN
    9781946764249 (Ebook) | ISBN 9781946764232 (hardcover)
Subjects: LCSH: Meditation.
Classification: LCC BF637.M4 (ebook) | LCC BF637.M4 O745 2018 (print) | DDC
    158.1/28--dc23
LC record available at https://lccn.loc.gov/2018010891

To the memory of María Luisa Führer, my mother

If there is a real desire,
if the thing desired is really light,
the desire for light produces it.
There is a real desire
when there is an effort of attention.
It is really light that is desired
if all other incentives are absent.
Even if our efforts of attention
seem for years to be producing no result,
one day a light which is in exact proportion to them
will flood the soul.
Every effort adds a little gold
to a treasure which no power on earth can take away.

SIMONE WEIL

1

I BEGAN TO SIT TO MEDITATE in silence and stillness on my own account and at my own risk, without anyone to give me any basic notions of how to do so or to accompany me in the process. The simplicity of the method—sitting, breathing, quieting one's thoughts—and most of all, the simplicity of its intention—to reconcile a person with what they are—seduced me from the beginning. As I have a tenacious temperament, I have remained faithful for several years to this discipline of simply sitting and gathering myself; and at once I understood that it was about accepting whatever came—whatever it might be—with good humor.

During the first few months I meditated badly, very badly; keeping my back straight and my knees bent was not at all easy for me and, as if that was not enough, I breathed with a certain agitation. I was perfectly aware that this sitting without doing anything was something as foreign to my education and experience as—contradictory though this seems—it was equally innate to who I was at my core. Nonetheless, there was something very powerful that pulled at me: the intuition that the path of silent meditation would guide me to encounter my own self at least as much or more so than literature, which I have always been very fond of.

For better or worse, since my earliest adolescence I have been someone very interested in delving into my own identity. That is why I've been an avid reader. That is why I studied philosophy and theology in my youth. The danger of an inclination of this type is, of course, self-centeredness; but thanks to sitting, breathing, and doing nothing else, I began to notice that this tendency could be eradicated not through the path of struggle and renunciation, as the Christian tradition that I belong to had taught me, but through the path of absurdity and exhaustion. Because all self-centeredness, including mine, when taken to its most radical extreme, demonstrates its ridiculousness and impracticability. Soon, thanks to meditation, even my narcissism displayed a positive side: thanks to it, I could persevere in my practice of silence and stillness. And having a good image of yourself is necessary for spiritual progress.

2

FOR THE FIRST YEAR, I was incredibly restless when I sat to meditate: my back hurt, my chest, my legs.... To tell the truth, almost everything hurt. Nonetheless, I soon noticed that there was practically never a moment when some part of my body did not hurt me; it was just that when I sat to meditate I became conscious of that pain. So I got in the habit of formulating questions: What hurts me? How does it hurt? And while I asked and attempted to answer myself, the truth was that the pain would disappear or simply change places. I did not take long to extract a lesson from this: pure observation is transformative. As Simone Weil—whom I began to read at that time—would say, there is no weapon more effective than attention.

The mental restlessness, which is what I perceived right after my physical discomfort, was no less a battle nor any more bearable an obstacle. On the contrary: an infinite boredom lay in wait for me during many of my sittings, as I began then to call them. I was tormented by the idea of getting stuck on some obsessive idea, which I was not sure how to eradicate, or on some disagreeable memory, which persisted in presenting itself just at the moment of my meditation. I breathed steadily, but my mind would be bombarded with some unfulfilled desire, with my guilt over one of my numerous mistakes, or with my recurrent fears, which tended to present themselves in new disguises each time. I fled all of this with considerable clumsiness; cutting short my periods of meditation, for example, or compulsively scratching my neck or nose—where an irritating itch frequently showed up. I also imagined scenes from my life that might have happened—I am very imaginative—turning over phrases for future texts, given that I am a writer; composing lists of pending chores; recalling incidents from the day; daydreaming about tomorrow.... Should I continue? I confirmed that remaining in silence with oneself is much more difficult than I had suspected before trying it. It did not take me long to come to a new conclusion: it was almost unbearable for me to be alone with myself, which was the reason why I constantly fled myself. This principle led me to the certainty that, as ample and rigorous as the analyses of my consciousness I had made during my decade of university education had been, my consciousness continued to be, after all that, a seldom frequented territory.

The sensation was that of someone writhing around in the mud. I had to wait some time for the clay to settle and the water to become clearer. But I am headstrong, as I have already said, and with the passage of the months I knew that when the water became clear, it would begin to fill with plants and fishes. I also knew that, with even more time and determination, these interior flora and fauna would grow richer the more they were observed. And now, as I write this account, I am amazed at how there once was so much mud where I now discover such varied and exuberant life.

3

BEFORE I DECIDED TO PRACTICE meditation with all the rigor I could, I had had so many experiences over the course of my life that I had reached a point where, without fear of exaggeration, I can say that I did not properly know who I was. I had traveled to many countries, read thousands of books, had an address book with hundreds of contacts, and had fallen in love with more women than I could remember. Like many of my contemporaries, I was convinced that the more experiences I had and the more intense and stunning they were, the sooner and better I would become a complete person. Today I know that that is not the case: the quantity of our experiences and their intensity serve only to bewilder us. Experiencing too many things tends to be prejudicial. I do not believe that humans are made for quantity, but rather for quality. Experiences, if one lives to collect too many of them, jostle us, they offer us utopian horizons, they inebriate and confuse us…. Now I would even say that any experience—even one that appears most innocent—tends to be too vertiginous for the human soul, which is only nourished by pausing the rhythm of the experiences it is offered.

Thanks to this initiation to reality that I have discovered with meditation, I know that the colorful fish that exist at the bottom of the ocean that is my consciousness, those interior flora and fauna that I have referred to above, can be seen only when the sea is calm, and not during the waves and storms of my experiences. And I also know that, when that sea is at an even greater calm, not even the fish can be made out, but just the water, water and nothing else. But human beings tend not to be satisfied with the fish, and even less with simply the water; we prefer the waves: they give us the impression of life, when the truth is that they are not life but just liveliness.

Today I know that it is a good idea to stop having experiences, whatever the genre, and to limit oneself to living: to allow life to express itself as it is, and not to fill it with the artifice of our travels or readings, relationships or passions, spectacles, entertainments, searches.... All of our experiences tend to compete with life and almost always manage to displace it and even cancel it out. True life is located behind what we call life. Not traveling, not reading, not talking: not doing these things is almost always better than doing them when it comes to the discovery of light and peace.

Of course, to discern something from all this that is written so quickly and understood so slowly I had to familiarize myself with my bodily sensations and, which is even more arduous, to classify my thoughts and feelings, my emotions. Because it is easy to say that one has distractions, but very difficult, on the other hand, to know from what type of distractions one suffers. It took me more than a year to begin to give a name to what appeared and disappeared from my mind when I sat to meditate. Until that moment I had been a spectator, yes, but hardly an attentive one. At the end of a sitting I could describe little of what had really happened to me during it.

To be attentive to the distractions themselves is more complicated than one imagines. In the first place because distractions, by their own evasive, nebulous nature, are not easily understandable; but also because in trying to retain them long enough to memorize and then be able to give an account of them, one winds up distracting oneself with that new activity. Despite all that, I could recognize and name a good part of my distractions and, thanks to this necessarily approximate typology, I could know, with significant precision, what level I had reached in my practice of meditation after a year and a half of assiduous perseverance.

4

AS UNTARNISHED AS MY INTEREST in silence and stillness was, it was clear to me that at any moment, before the least mishap or adversity, I might give up on what I had decided was my most crucial spiritual practice. And it must be said that I would have some good reasons for abandoning it: the pain in my knees, for example (a traumatologist strongly advised me against the posture in which I meditated), the loss of time (my work piled up), the impossibility of training a body shaped by forty years of bad posture (I began to visit a chiropractor), the lack of results. After all, and I asked myself this question many times, what had I really gotten after hundreds of hours dedicated to simply sitting and breathing? I still did not realize that resistance to the practice is the same thing as resistance to life.

Judging from the little that my meditation practice tidied up my life and by the great sacrifice that it entailed, everything pointed toward my leaving it aside—in one way or another, sooner or later—to devote myself to activities that I then considered to be more beneficial. Against all odds, I persevered, I inexplicably persevered; and if it is true that the power of an ideal can be great, the power of reality—when one is in front of it, when one can feel it—is mysteriously so much greater.

To strengthen my conviction and support my willpower, I focused on what I considered to be most crucial: silence. I refer as much to what exists in silence as to silence itself, which is an authentic revelation. From here I must nonetheless issue a warning that silence, at least as I have lived it, is nothing special. Silence is only the frame and context that makes everything else possible. And what is everything else? The surprising thing is that it is not anything, absolutely nothing: life itself going by, nothing special. Of course I say "nothing," but I could also say "everything."

For someone like me, Western down to my medulla, it was a great achievement to understand, and to begin to experience, that I could exist without thinking, without planning, without imagining, to exist without making the most of things, without producing: to be in the world, to merge into it, a worldly being and the world itself, without the Cartesian divisions or distinctions that I was so accustomed to because of my education.

5

ALL OF THIS, which has come very slowly, has been accompanied by signs such as a growing love for nature, fondness for the mountains, the ever more urgent need to withdraw for several days in solitude, the significant diminution of my reading—a passion that had turned into a vice—greater care for my diet, and some new friendships. But as I am a seasoned explorer of my consciousness, as I began perceiving all of these changes I could not resist the temptation to take note of them, so that I could witness, with an even greater consciousness, the transformation of this biography, something I want to recount, although succinctly, in this brief, testimonial essay.

I have the conviction that I have designed a spiritual path, which I am attempting to explain on these pages. This is not to say that I have not been oriented by illuminating readings or that I have not received pertinent instructions from meditation teachers; I have admired the tenacity of other seekers in silence, alongside whom I have journeyed some distance. But in every case my impression is that it has been I and only I who have walked—guided by my inner teacher—to where I find myself now.

For me, the best indication that I was sitting better each time was that I always wanted to sit more. Because the more you sit to meditate, the more you want to sit. I have even come to believe that sometimes the most natural thing for humans to do is just to meditate. It is true that at the beginning everything seemed more important to me than meditating; but the moment has come when sitting and not doing anything other than being in contact with my own self, present to my present, seems like the most important thing of all. We normally live scattered—that is to say, outside of ourselves. Meditation concentrates us, brings us back home, and teaches us to live together with our own being. Without this living together with oneself, without our being centered on what we really are, I find a humane and dignified life to be very difficult, if not impossible.

Nonetheless, here I cannot disguise the fact that I seek too many things in life, which means that there is still too little acceptance. Because I greatly fear that when we seek we tend to reject what we already have. Having said that, all authentic seeking ends by bringing us back to where we were. The finger that points outward ends up pointing back at ourselves.

6

IT HAS COST ME four decades to comprehend that people begin to live to the degree to which they quit dreaming of themselves. That we begin to bear fruit when we stop building castles in the air. That there is nothing that does not have its stock in reality. The more one familiarizes oneself with reality, whatever it may be, the better. Just as the child who is learning to ride a bicycle falls to the ground when they stop to consider how well or poorly they are riding, and actually manages to ride it when they are most deeply submerged in the activity, so are we, all of us, best when submerged in any activity that we undertake. As soon as we begin to judge the results, life's magic evaporates and we are knocked over, no matter how high or low our flight was. This is, in essence, what meditation teaches: to submerge oneself in what one is doing. "When I eat, I eat; when I sleep, I sleep," as it is said one great master defined Zen. With this spirit, it is not just that one devotes less energy to the development of a certain activity, but that one also leaves the activity invigorated. The human being has the potential to recharge itself in action.

I will illustrate what I intend to say. Like the novelist that I am, I have known which pages of my books were inspired and which ones were not since I was very young. Deep down, it is very easy to find it out: the inspired ones are those that I have written when I have forgotten myself, submerged in the writing, abandoned to its fate; the less inspired ones, by contrast, are those I have worked over most, those I have planned and edited in a more rational and less intuitive manner. That is why I think that to write, like to live or to love, one should not hold on, but rather let oneself loose; not restrain oneself, but rather let go. The key to almost everything is in the magnanimity of release. Love, art, and meditation—at least these three things work that way.

When I say that it is a good idea to be loose or detached I refer to the importance of trust. The more trust a human being has in another, the better they will be able to love the other; the more a creator gives to the work, the more it is repaid. Love—like art or meditation—is pure and simple trust. And practice too, of course, because trust is exercised.

Meditation is a discipline to increase trust. We sit and then what do we do? We trust. Meditation is a practice of waiting. But what is really being waited for? Nothing and everything. If one waits on something concrete, that waiting will be worthless, as it will be inspired by the desire for the thing that is lacked. But when the waiting is neither utilitarian nor free, it turns into something real and genuinely spiritual.

All of us have the experience of how boring and uncomfortable waiting tends to be. As a practice in the art of waiting, meditation tends to be quite boring. So, what great faith one must have to sit in silence and stillness! Everything is a question of faith. If you have faith when you sit to meditate, the more you sit, the more your faith will grow. So that I could say that I meditate in order to have faith in meditation. Though I may appear inactive, when I am sitting I better understand that the world does not depend on me; things are as they are independent of my intervention. This insight is very healthy: it places me, as a human being, in a humbler position—it un-centers me and offers me a mirror just my size.

7

TO TURN MYSELF into someone who meditates, aside from sitting down for one, two, or three periods of some twenty or twenty-five minutes every day, I did not have to do anything special. It all consisted of being what I had been up to that point—but consciously, attentively. All my effort had to be limited to controlling the comings and goings of my mind, putting my imagination in my employ, and stopping myself from being its servant. Because if we are in truth masters of our faculties, why do we behave ourselves like servants?

Attention was driving me toward wonder. In reality, the more we let ourselves marvel at what happens—that is to say, the more we are children—the more we grow as people. Meditation—and I like this—helps us recover our lost childhood. If all that I live and see does not surprise me it is because, as it is emerging—or even before—I have subjugated it to a bias or a particular way of thinking, thus making it impossible for all of its potential to be displayed before me.

It is very rare, certainly, for a capacity for wonder to remain in an activity that we repeat on a daily basis or even several times a day. That is why it is necessary to train. Everything plays out in perception, that is what one discovers when one's training is continued and correct. It is finally understood that we can only be happy when we perceive what is real. I will give an example.

After finishing my last intensive meditation retreat (I devote a full day once a month entirely to this activity), I went to walk in the mountains and for a few moments—perhaps an hour—I experienced a deep and unusual bliss. Everything seemed very beautiful, radiant to me, and I had the sensation, which is difficult to explain, that it was not me who was on that mountain, but that the mountain was me. Afternoon fell, and the sky was cloudy, but I felt that the day was perfectly beautiful just as it was. Because of the amount of sitting I had done that day, my right knee hurt a bit; but that pain, strangely, didn't bother me. I would almost say that I found it a little funny and that I accepted it without resisting it. Laska, my dog, jumped between the rocks and ran back and forth.

Seeing him, I thought that my dog lives intensely at every second; by observing him a lot, as he is a faithful companion, I have concluded that at least in that respect I want to resemble him. I live with an animal to nurture the animal that exists in me. Now I understand that.

My sensation of effervescent bliss during that hike through the mountain disappeared eventually, but thanks to it I believe I now have a closer idea of the happiness I aspire to. At this moment, for example, I am writing next to the fireplace in my house. Laska is at my feet and I am listening to the rain falling outside: I cannot imagine greater abundance. Wood to burn, books to read, wine to savor, and friends with whom to share all this. There is not much missing for true happiness.

A few days after that retreat I returned to the same mountain, but it was no longer the same. In truth, it was me who was no longer the same. We cannot track down past happiness, that is absurd. And from all this experience, what have I concluded? That happiness is essentially perception. And that if we limit ourselves to perceiving, we will finally arrive at what we are.

8

THE MORE WE MEDITATE, the greater our capacity for perception and the finer our sensitivity, I can guarantee that. One quits living dully, which is how our days tend to go by otherwise. The gaze is cleansed and the true color of things can begin to be seen. The ear is tuned to unexpected extremes, and you begin to hear—and there is not an ounce of poetry in this— the true sound of the world. Everything, even the most prosaic things, seems more brilliant and simple. You walk with a lighter step. You smile more frequently. The atmosphere seems filled with some something, essential and burning. Does that sound good? Excellent! But I confess that I have only experienced it for several seconds and only on a handful of occasions.

Normally I am adrift: between the man I was before I began with meditation and the one I am beginning to be now. "Adrift" is the most precise description: sometimes here, meditating, sometimes who knows where, there where my uncountable distractions have taken me. I am something like a boat, and more a fragile raft than a solid transatlantic liner. The waves play with me at their whim, but from so much watching how those waves come and go, the truth is that I myself am beginning to transform into the waves and to not know what has become of my poor raft. Until, indeed, I find it: "Yes, there it is," I tell myself then. "Adrift." Each time I board that raft, I stop being myself; each time that I fling myself into the sea, I find myself.

9

ONE OF THE FIRST FRUITS of my meditation practice was intuiting how nothing in this world stays stable. I already knew that everything changes—it's obvious— but upon meditating I began to experience it. We also change, despite how much we insist on seeing ourselves as something permanent or durable. This essential mutability of the human being and of things is—this is how I see it now—a piece of good news.

The curious thing is that this discovery came to me by means of stillness. Everything happened as I will now explain: upon meditating I confirm that when I lingered on one of my thoughts, it faded (something that certainly did not happen when I looked at a person, whose consistency is independent of my attention). As I understand it, this demonstrates that thoughts are scarcely trustworthy, whereas people, on the contrary, even if only because they have a body, are quite a bit more so. I decided that, from then on, I would not put my trust in something that faded so easily. I decided to let myself be guided by what remains, as only that is worthy of my trust. What do I put my trust in? This is, I sense, the great question.

Accepting this constant mutability of the world and of oneself is not an easy task, principally because it makes any closed definition unfeasible. Human beings tend to define ourselves by contrast or in opposition, which is the same as saying by separation and division. In dividing, separating, and opposing we distance ourselves from our very selves. Defining a person and not accepting their radical mutability is like putting an animal in a cage. A caged lion is not a lion, but a caged lion; and that is a very different thing.

From my present—and I am trying to be concrete—I cannot condemn who I was in the past for the simple reason that the man I now judge and disapprove of is a different person from who I am now. We always act according to the wisdom that we have at that moment, and if we act poorly it is because, at least at that point, there was ignorance. It is absurd to condemn past ignorance from the place of present wisdom.

10

THE MORE WE SEE our radical mutability and our inter-dependence with the world and with others—up to the point of being able to say "I am you" or even "I am the universe"—the more we approach our most radical identity. To know oneself, therefore, one does not have to divide or separate, but to unite. Thanks to meditation I have continued to discover that there is not I and world, but that world and I are one same, sole thing. The natural consequence of such a discovery—and I do not think one has to be very sharp to guess this—is compassion toward every living being; you do not want to do harm to anything or anyone because you notice that you would harm yourself if you did so. The tree cannot be cut with impunity, without asking its permission. The earth cannot be removed from one place to be used in another without paying some price. Everything that you do to other beings and to nature you do to yourself. Through meditation, the mystery of unity continues to reveal itself to me.

Of course, you do not get to scuba dive in the ocean of unity without splashing about for a long time in the pools of division. If water does not flow it stagnates and smells bad; we all know that. All life that does not flow rots and smells bad too. Our life is worthy of that name only if it flows, if it is in motion. Because of cowardice or laziness or even inertia—although it is almost always fear that most paralyzes us—we all tend to stay still and, furthermore, to dig our heels in. Digging our heels in is not just staying still; it makes any future motion more difficult. We seek jobs that reassure us, marriages that reassure us, firm, clear ideas, conservative parties, and rites that give us back a sense of continuity.... We seek protected residences, well-covered health care, and low-risk investments. We play it safe and that is how the river of our life encounters obstacles on its course, until one day, without prior warning, it stops flowing. We are alive, yes, but we are very often dead. We have survived ourselves: there is bio-logy, but not bio-graphy.

11

THANKS TO MY MEDITATION PRACTICE I have discovered that everything—without exception—can be an adventure. Writing a novel, cultivating a friendship, or taking a trip is an adventure. But taking a walk can be an adventure too, and so can reading a story or making dinner. In reality, even the grayest day is an incommensurate adventure for one who knows how to live it. Making the bed, cleaning the dishes, going shopping, taking the dog out … and so many other common chores are everyday adventures, but not any less exciting and even dangerous because of that. My meditation points out the adventurous—which is the same as saying extraordinary or miraculous—character of the ordinary.

What really kills us is routine and what saves us is creativity, that is to say, the capacity to glimpse and reclaim novelty. If properly seen—and that is what meditation teaches—everything is always new and different. Absolutely nothing is now as it was an instant ago. Participating in this continuous change that we call "life," being one with it, is the only sensible promise of happiness.

For that reason, it is not important if you sit well or poorly to meditate. Whatever mood one is in—happy or sad, hopeful or disillusioned—is the best possible mood at that moment for meditating, precisely because it is the mood that you are in. Thanks to meditation, you learn to not want to go to any place other than where you are; you want to be in the mood you are in, but fully, to explore it and to see how deep it goes.

To realize that any mood, even those that seem more authentic and unquestionable, is fleeting is all one has to do to confirm that everything inside of us is born and dies with an astonishing ease. Meditation consists precisely of attending to the birth and death of all of this as a spectator, on the stage of our consciousness. Where does what dies go? I have asked myself a thousand times. Where does what is born in the mind come from? What is there between the death of one thing and the birth of another thing? This is the space in which I feel that I should reside; this is the space where perennial wisdom buds.

From the times that I have discerned something of this space and when I have inhabited it, even if just for a few seconds, I can assure you that true happiness is something very simple, and that it is in reach of all of us, of anyone. You just have to stop, shut up, listen, and look; although stopping, shutting up, listening, and looking—and that is meditating—is so difficult for us today and we have had to invent a method for something so elemental. Meditation is not difficult; the difficult thing is wanting to meditate.

12

BEING CONSCIOUS CONSISTS of contemplating your thoughts. Consciousness is unity with yourself. When I am conscious, I return to my home; when I lose my consciousness, I go away, to who knows where? All thoughts and ideas distance us from ourselves. You are what remains when your thoughts disappear. Of course, I do not believe that it is possible to live without any type of thought. Because no matter how much meditation you do, thoughts—and it is not good to forget this—can never be fully calmed. They will always survive, but our attachment to them quiets down and, with it, their frequency and intensity diminishes.

I would go even further: you should not be conscious of what you think or do, but rather simply think or do it. Being conscious already assumes an opening in what we do or think. The secret is to live fully in what you have between your hands. So that, as strange as it seems, exercising the consciousness is the way to live placidly without it: totally now, totally here.

13

DESPITE WHAT I JUST WROTE, I recognize that I spend a good portion of my sittings daydreaming; I also recognize that I typically find that dreaming quite agreeable. But I do not fool myself: that is not meditation. It seems like meditation, but it is not. Because meditation is not about daydreaming, but about being awake. Dreaming is escaping, and it is not necessary to be always escaping to live. The difficulty is in how much we like our dreams, how drunk we get on them. We live inebriated on ideas and ideals, confusing life and fantasy. Beneath its prosaic appearance, life, any life, is much more beautiful and intense than the best of fantasies. My actual partner, for example, is much more beautiful than the marvelous idea that I can have of her. My actual novel is infinitely better than any imagined novel, among other reasons because that imagined novel does not even exist. It takes a lot to accept it, but there is nothing as pernicious as an ideal and nothing as liberating as a reality, whatever it might be.

The good thing about meditation is that, in virtue of my continued exercise, I began to shed everything fanciful from my life and to keep only what is real. Like the art that it is, meditation loves the concrete and refutes the abstract. The one who abandons the illusion of dreams, enters the country of reality. And reality is full of real smells and textures, of real colors and flowers. Of course, reality can be graceless or excessive, but it never disappoints. Dreams, on the other hand, do disappoint us. Further still: the nature of dreams, their essence, is precisely deception. Dreams always escape: they are evanescent, ungraspable. Reality, on the other hand, does not flee; it is us who flee from it. Meditating is throwing oneself headfirst into reality and taking a bath in the self.

Romantic love, as an example, tends to be very false: no one lives more deceived than someone in love, and few suffer as much. Authentic love has little to do with falling in love, which is today the dream par excellence, the only myth remaining in the West. In authentic love, nothing is expected from the other; in romantic love, it is. More still: romantic love is essentially the hope that our partner will bring us happiness. When we fall in love, we overburden the other with our expectations. And so great are these expectations that finally practically nothing remains of our beloved. The other, then, is simply an excuse, a screen for our expectations. That is why one tends to move so quickly from falling in love to hate or indifference, because no one can fulfill such monstrous expectations.

Our society's exaltation of romantic love has caused and continues to cause bottomless wells of unhappiness. The present idealization of the couple is a pernicious stupidity. Of course I believe in the possibility of love with a partner, but I am convinced that it requires an extraordinary and uncommon maturity. No one close to us can ever provide the radical security that we seek; they cannot and should not give it. The beloved being is not there to keep one from getting lost, but so that the couple can live the liberating adventure of being lost together.

14

JUST LIKE ALMOST the entire human population, I spend my time chasing what brings me pleasure and rejecting what makes me feel bad. I am a little fed up with living this way: attracted or repelled, running after something or, on the other hand, keeping as much distance as possible. An existence that passes by taking and condemning winds up being exhausting, and I ask myself if it would not be possible to live without imposing our preferences or aversions on life. That is precisely what meditation calls me to: to not impose my own likes or dislikes on life, to allow reality to express itself, and to contemplate it without the lenses of my aversions or affinities. It is about having the receptacle that I am as clean as possible, the way that water can be seen for all its purity when it is poured out. It would be stupendous to see something without aspirations, freely, without the perspective of what it could be for me. It is possible, there are people who have done it. Why not me?

More than being one with the world, what we want is for the world to submit to our appetites. We spend our lives manipulating things and people so that they please us. That constant violence, that insatiable search which does not even pause at the misfortune of others, that compulsive and structural greed is what destroys us. The happiness of meditation (or just happiness, why qualify it?) resides in not manipulating and limiting oneself to being what can be seen, heard, or touched.

I like it or I don't like it: that is how we tend to divide the world, exactly as a child would. That classification is not just egocentric, but radically impoverishing and, ultimately, unjust. As widespread as it is to live pursuing whatever pleases us and avoiding whatever displeases us, such a lifestyle makes life somewhat exhausting. What displeases us has its right to exist; what displeases us can even do us good and, in that sense, it does not seem intelligent to escape from it. With its disagreeable appearance, what displeases us has a necessary core. By means of meditation one tries to enter that marrow and, at the very least, wet one's lips with its nectar.

15

EVERYTHING CAN SERVE to build or to destroy and so, in this sense, anything is worthy of meditation. By virtue of my faith in the healing power of silence, at first I believed that I could fix almost everything in me that did not work, sooner or later, with my sittings. Little by little I perceived that the sittings pointed toward things outside of the sittings themselves and that, as a result, anything that I heard, observed, or did served to qualify my meditation and definitely to strengthen my character. Paying more attention while I was brushing my teeth, for example, I was able to perceive the flow of water, its refreshing contact with my hands, the way

I turn off the tap, the weave of the towel I use to dry my hands…. Each sensation, as minimal as it seems, is worthy of being explored. Enlightenment (that is, that light which occasionally turns on in our interior, helping us to understand life) hides in the most diminutive acts and can arrive at any moment and through any circumstance. Living well means being always in contact with oneself, something only tiring when considered intellectually and something that can actually be restful and renewing when indeed it takes place.

A writer—I use examples that are close to me—is not just a writer when he creates his work, but always. A seeker, an explorer of interior abysses, is not just that when she sits to meditate, but always. The quality of meditation is proven in life itself, that is the test. That is why no meditation should be judged by how we have sat through it, but by the fruits that it yields. Moreover, meditation and life should move toward being the same thing. I meditate so that my life becomes meditation; I live so that my meditation becomes my life. I do not aspire to contemplate, but to be a contemplative being, which is to live without craving.

16

MEDITATION MAKES POSSIBLE those fleeting but undoubtable glimpses of the real that are occasionally gifted to us: moments when we perceive who we are in reality and why we are in this world. We perceive this on rare occasions in a non-verbal, incomprehensible intuition. Before long it becomes evident to us that we are this way, and though we cannot articulate it, we seek for that intuition to be repeated so that we can return to that primordial being that we truly are and which, because of circumstance, because of all the noise, has been clouded over or even forgotten. I ask myself, "What has happened that we have so lost ourselves? How is it that I do not know that which should be familiar to me?" Questions and questions about paradise lost. Well then, the answer to these questions is in the place where they are born. As long as humans have questions to ask themselves, they still have salvation.

To reach these glimpses of the real, it is not worth the pain of making an effort. Rather than helping find what is sought, effort tends to make seeking more difficult. It is not a good idea to resist, but to surrender. Not to endeavor, but to live with abandon. Both art and meditation are born from surrendering, not from effort. Love is the same. Effort puts will and reason to work; surrendering, in contrast, employs freedom and intuition. Of course, we could well ask ourselves how one can surrender without effort. The Chinese have a concept for this: wu wei, to do without doing. Wu wei consists of putting yourself in a disposition that allows for something to happen through your meditation, but not doing it yourself directly, forcing its start, development, or culmination. The only thing necessary for that surrender is being there, to thus perceive whatever appears, whatever it may be. Meditation is a rigorous training for surrender.

We do not have to make anything up, we have only to receive what life has made up for us; and then, it is true, give it to others. The great teachers are—and here there are no exceptions—great receivers.

17

I VERY MUCH LIKE to take a small bow before the cushion or stool that I am going to sit on to meditate, as well as the small altar that presides over the oratory or meditation room. I like this gesture because with it I express my respect toward the space in which I most work on my inner adventure. Respect to me is the first sign of love. By means of frequent gassho, or small reverences typical of Buddhist practice, Zen teaches respect for reality. And reality will not be respected if it is not ultimately considered mysterious. Meditation helps one comprehend that everything is a mystery and that, because of that, everything is capable of causing a genuinely religious attitude. For the person who meditates—today I see it this way—there is no distinction between the sacred and the profane.

All the characteristic prostrations of Zen Buddhism can surely drive the gesture to mechanical repetition, that is, to emptying the gesture of its content, reducing it to pure form. That degeneration is what we know as routine. But all of these prostrations can also drive one toward the great question of the prostrate: to what or whom do I actually prostrate myself in life? Or, said differently, what or who is truly my God, and which are my idols?

During meditation I can reverently bow before the stool or cushion, but in my ordinary life it is not unusual for me to do so before my professional prestige, which I care for as if it were the most delicate of plants; or before my bank account, whose movements I control with a revealing frequency; or before the characteristic well-being of a comfortable well-off life, for which I spare no expense. Enthusiastic about my ritual prostrations or ignorant of how existential prostrations are the ones that really count, I have discovered in meditation how limited and crude that form of conducting myself is. I have splashed around in that mud a lot—I admit it—and what should I have done? Not judge myself, that is clear; and much less condemn myself. It is absolutely unnecessary to judge, it is enough to observe; simple observation is effective for change. In truth, the capacity of observation—what Simone Weil calls attention—is the mother of all virtues.

18

WE WOULD GAIN a lot if instead of passing judgment on things, we faced up to them. Our mental speculation does not just make us lose very precious time, but because of it we also lose the opportunity to transform ourselves. Because there are things that can no longer be done if they are not done at a particular moment or that, at least, cannot be done as they should have been.

Personally, I am convinced that more than eighty percent of our mental activity—and it is likely that I have underestimated that proportion—is totally irrelevant and dispensable, and even counterproductive. It is much healthier to think less and trust more in our intuition, our first impulse. When we reflect, we tend to complicate things that otherwise seem sharp and clear at the first moment. Almost no reflection moves to action; most reflection leads to paralysis. We reflect to paralyze ourselves, to find a motive to justify our inaction. We think life a lot, but we live it little. That is my sad balance.

None of this means that thinking is bad, but that it is good only in its right measure. Thinking is like sleeping or eating: done in excess it runs the risk of stupefying us. Just as when we sit down at the table to eat at a set time—we do not eat in any way or at any hour—perhaps when it comes to thinking we should also sit down and do it intentionally, not just do it whenever it is convenient. Thinking, like any human activity, should be preceded by an act of will. That is what makes it human. The more you think, the more you should meditate: that is the rule. Why that? Because the more we fill our head with words, the greater our need to empty it to leave it clean again.

19

ALL OF THIS is very difficult to share and, possibly, to understand, because in the West we live in a world that is too intellectualized. To face up to that generalized and exacerbated intellectualism it is necessary to awaken the inner teacher that each of us has inside of ourselves and, in short, let them speak. I say this because at our core we are all much wiser than we believe and because at that core we all know well what it is that is expected of us and what we should do. The inner teacher does not tell us anything we do not already know; the inner teacher reminds us of what we do know and places us before the evidence so that we smile. To tell the truth, none of the teachers in the world are necessary: each being is an entire cosmos of knowledge and wisdom.

That smile that I just mentioned, indulgent and benevolent, is infinitely more effective, in the face of transformation itself, than any condemnation or reprimand. The child whose mischief is time and time again discovered stops doing it. Bad habits are demolished in meditation by pure observation and by means of a friendly smile. To see and to smile, that is the key to transformation.

Smiling at suffering can seem excessive. But the truth is that sadness and misfortune are there for our growth. The bad must be accepted, which means being able to see its good side and, all things considered, appreciate it. We know that we have accepted suffering when we have extracted something good from it and, consequently, we have given thanks for having endured it. I am not saying that smiling before adversity is the most spontaneous thing; but it is without doubt the most intelligent and sensible response. And I will explain why. Reacting to pain with animosity turns it into suffering. Smiling before it, in contrast, neutralizes its venom. No one is going to argue that pain is disagreeable, but accepting the disagree-ableness and surrendering yourself to it without resistance is the way for it to become less disagree-able. What makes us suffer is our resistance to reality.

20

AT EVERY MOMENT I have a dilemma to resolve: do I stay here, where I am, or do I go elsewhere? Do I remain with myself or do I leave and distance myself from myself? Since starting meditation, I choose to remain at home more often and not to flee. Losing consciousness and traveling to who knows where would seem to be much more fatiguing than staying alert; but for me that is still not the case: attention seems like work, and distraction, by contrast, like a rest. All of these resistances on my part are absurd and have a very clear cause: the foolish belief that by losing my ghosts I will end up losing myself. But my ghosts are not me; they are the least me-thing that exists inside me.

This has taken me years of meditation practice to discover. But today I know, and I say it with as much pride as humility, that connecting with pain itself and with the pain of the world is the only demonstrable form of demolishing the first of one's idols, which is none other than one's own well-being. To achieve such a connection with pain it is necessary to do just the opposite of what we have been taught: not to run, but to pause; not to make an effort, but to abandon oneself; not to propose goals, but simply to be there.

After saying that, it is worth affirming that pain is our principal teacher. The lesson of reality—which is the only lesson worth listening to—cannot be learned without pain. Meditation for me does not have anything to do with a hypothetical state of placidness, as so many understand it. Rather it has to do with ceasing to struggle with pain. Meditation is, therefore, the art of surrender. In the fight that is each sitting, the victor is the one who surrenders to reality. If we are taught in the world to close ourselves off to pain, in meditation we are taught to open ourselves to it. Meditation is a school of opening to reality.

Given what I have written above, it is not surprising that silent meditation and stillness have been accused of sophisticated masochism. The fact is that one arrives at a point at which one wishes to sit daily with the right portion of pain: to frequent it, to know it, and to domesticate it.... Without ceasing to exist, pain changes direction depending on how often it is frequented. And that is how one learns to be with oneself.

21

IT'S CURIOUS TO HAVE evidence that something that should be so basic is for many of us in fact so difficult. What must be learned urgently is that we are not gods, that we cannot—nor should we—subject life to our whims: it is not the world that should adjust to our desires, but rather our desires that should adjust to the possibilities that the world offers. For all these reasons, meditation is a school of initiation to adult life: a waking up to what we are.

We human beings are characterized by an excessive eagerness for possessing things, ideas, people.... We are insatiable! The less we are, the more we want to have. Meditation teaches, in contrast, that when one has nothing the self is given more opportunities. It is in nothingness that the being shines in all its splendor. That's why it is good once and for all to quit desiring and accumulating things; it is good to begin to open the gifts that life gives us, and then immediately afterwards simply to enjoy them. Meditation pacifies the machine of desire and encourages enjoyment of what we already have. Because everything, anything, is there for our growth and delight. The more we desire and accumulate, the further we move away from the source of happiness. Stop! Look! That is what I hear in my meditation. And if I heed the command and indeed stop and look then—ah!—the miracle happens.

We almost never notice that the problem that worries us tends not to be our real problem. The authentic, burning, untouched problem always hides behind the obvious problem. The solutions we have for our obvious problems are always completely useless, given that they are also obvious. We go from false problem to false problem, and from false solution to false solution. We destroy the tip of the iceberg and we think that we have eliminated the entire thing. Do you want to know your iceberg? That is the most interesting question. It is not difficult: it is enough to quit writhing in the waves and begin to scuba dive. It is enough to hold your breath and put your head beneath the water. Once you are there, it is enough to open your eyes and see.

However big our iceberg is—any iceberg—it is just water. It only takes a sufficiently powerful heat source for it to dissolve. Ice always dissolves with heat. It may take a long time if the iceberg is large, but it will dissolve if we keep that heat source working and close. The only thing missing is a true curiosity to know the iceberg itself. The more one observes oneself, the more what we believe crumbles and the less we know who we are. One must remain in that ignorance, endure it, befriend it, accept that we are lost and that we have been drifting, directionless. It is possible that we have lost time, even life, but these losses have driven us to where we now are, to the point of sitting to meditate. Meditating is placing oneself exactly in this precise instant: you have been a vaga-bond, but you can become a pilgrim. Do you want to?

22

WAKING UP IS DISCOVERING that we are in a jail. But waking up is also discovering that this jail has no bars and that, strictly speaking, it is not properly a jail. We begin to ask ourselves, why have I lived locked in a jail with no bars? And we go to its door. And we walk out. Meditating is that moment that we exit. We discover that the door has never been closed, that it is we who have closed it with a double turn of the key. That door is not a door—we invented it. "The gateless gate" is a typically Zen phrase that makes me think that a good part of what we consider to be our life is purely illusory: loveless love, friendless friendship, artless art, religionless religion....

So now stop looking at that door that you have created and get up and open it. Better still, get up and realize that there is no door. To a large extent, we can do what we want and if we do not do it, it is precisely because we do not understand or do not want to understand something so basic.

It is good to very slowly study the material with which we have made the bars of our jail. And we also have to study the process by which these bars are made. The spark or intuition that frees us is made possible through studying what imprisons us. To live in reality, we must demolish the dreams that have jailed us. Our dreams are generally not truly ours: we borrow them or fabricate them out of an untrustworthy material. Whether we investigate our lives or not, almost all dreams will end up crumbling precisely because they are not ours.

23

IN REALITY, THERE is no absolute problem. We do not have a problem, and much less are we a problem ourselves. We like problems because they give us the impression that thanks to them we are able to exist. The true problem is that our problems are false. We can be happy; at our core, we can only be so. We have believed that our problems were us and so it is difficult to leave them behind. We fear losing ourselves, but we should lose ourselves. When we do not grab onto anything, we float away.

At the end of the day, no problem is more than an idea that I have about certain situations. The situation—whatever it is—is not the real problem: the idea is. Inasmuch as I abandon the idea, the problem disappears. Not having ideas about things or situations is enough to live completely happily. The formula for happiness is to take things as they are, not how we would like them to be, to swim with life's current, rather than against it. One does not even have to swim. It is enough to open one's arms and let oneself be taken away. Whatever shore that current takes you to is good for you; this is faith. You are your main obstacle. Quit being your own obstacle now. Remove yourself from the middle of things as much as you can and, simply, you will begin to discover the world.

24

IF WE WERE TO CONSIDER for a moment that all the difficulties that it is our turn to pass through in this stage of our life are opportunities that destiny—that friend—offers us to grow, would we not see everything in a different way? That colleague who badmouthed you, for example; or that pending work that should have been finished months ago; or that appointment with the doctor that you postpone again and again.... It would not be strange for you to identify with some of these examples: we human beings resemble each other, we all suffer the same things. So all of these, which at first glance appear to be problems, in the light of meditation begin to look like opportunities. The time has come to put that badmouthing colleague in place; that pending task has turned out much more tolerable than you imagined; the doctor has discovered another illness that you can now prevent.... In brief, life's great hurdles are what most make us grow. We should be grateful to have so many conflicts!

We can consider what life offers us as obstacles, but it is more reasonable and healthier to consider them as opportunities for advancement. Inasmuch as we welcome suffering, it loses its venom, and turns into something much purer, more innocuous, and, at the same time, more intense. It is always smarter to face a problem or danger directly than to hide or flee from it. If something rears its head in our life, whatever it is, the best thing to do is to face up to it as soon as possible, to know whom or what we must deal with.

We always think that the problem is outside of us: it's my boss's fault, or my partner's, the country's economy.... We attribute our lack of faith to the

mediocrity of our religious representatives, the dys-
function of our neighborhood or city to the egoism
and charlatanism of our politicians, and the failure of
our marriage to a third person that got in our way.…
It is incredible, our ability to blame our work for our
lack of creativity, our parents for a negative feature
of our character, or our children for our renunciation of any personal aspirations. Meditation turns the
finger that points at everyone else back around until
it points at us. Let us admit that the accusing finger
becomes uncomfortable. What is true is that all our
perceived problems, absolutely all of them, depend
on ourselves to an enormous degree. That is why the
meditation that I am writing about here, because of
its depth, requires an ever-greater maturity: the ability to assume proper responsibility. Initiating yourself
in meditation means arriving at a place where you no
longer tolerate pointing at circumstances or blaming
others. When you reach this point is when you should
sit to meditate.

25

IT'S WONDERFUL TO NOTICE how we achieve great changes in the most absolute stillness. Because it is not just silence that is curative, but stillness as well. For it must be said that silence in stillness is very different from silence in movement. It is scientifically demonstrated that motionless eyes provide the subject with a greater concentration than eyes in movement. While moving, it is very easy, almost inevitable, to be outside ourselves. Stillness, on the other hand, invites interiorization. It is necessary to pass through stillness to train oneself to master it, without which true freedom cannot be discussed.

Sitting in stillness turns out to be so arduous because of the exalted and disproportionate image that we tend to have of ourselves. The immaturity or infantilism of some adults is nothing more than the loss of a sense of proportion. In meditation, we place each thing in its place and we discover what our place is: a place that we certainly despised and branded contemptible before the practice of silence in stillness; but also a place that, once seen, one does not wish to abandon.

Since I discovered the power of meditation, I began to discretely display the vulnerability that characterizes us humans, which I had so tried to hide from the world. That modest display of my weaknesses has revealed itself as a very effective way to acknowledge the worship of my own image that I had lived with up to that point. Showing vulnerability is the only way that allows others to truly know us, and, consequently, to love us.

In one way or another, when meditating one works with the material of vulnerability itself. We always have the impression that we are starting from zero: the house itself never seems to be built; we feel we are just permanently reinforcing the foundation. In meditation there is not, at least by appearances, a significant shift from one place to another; rather there is a sort of installation in a non-place. That non-place is the now, the instant is the instance.

26

THE POWERFUL ATTRACTIVENESS that sexuality exercises over humans comes down, precisely, to the power of the now. The most consumed lovers are inside each other in that eternal present when their bodies and souls are surrendered to one other. The erotic experience can be so intense that it does not allow escape either to the past or to the future: that is its enchantment, its attractiveness. It is the same enchantment of authentic meditation and of any activity undertaken with total surrender.

When we surrender ourselves completely to what we do, nothing is burdensome and everything seems light to us. One lets oneself feel the burden when they stop surrendering. Any activity undertaken with concentration is the source of an indescribable happiness. Artistic creation, for example, is good if it produces joy. In this sense, it is not at all true that one must make an effort or discipline oneself to write a book. The book writes itself, the painting paints itself, and the writer or the painter is there, before their blank canvas or notebook, while that happens. The writer's virtue resides only in being there when the book is written, that is all.

27

AFTER GREAT THOUGHT, I have concluded that what I most like about meditating is that it is a space—a time—free of drama. Those who do not meditate like, generally, to live with emotions; those who meditate, in contrast, like to live without them. In meditation, one discovers that one does not have to add anything to life for it to be life and, even more so, that everything we add to it numbs it.

Lamentably, we all tend to be too enamored with drama. As much as we perceive ourselves as nondramatic beings, we get bored of ourselves! We invent problems and difficulties to season our biographies, which appear flat and gray to us without these obstacles. Discovering that one cannot undertake a certain task, for example, does not have to be a problem; it can be a freedom. The convalescence that an illness entails can be lived as a well-deserved season of vacation. The rupture of a marriage can be the first step toward a better marriage. Put more simply: the bitterness or sweetness of life does not depend on reality—marriage, task, or illness—but rather on us, only us. Thanks to meditation I have discovered that no burden is mine if I do not hoist it onto my shoulders.

28

THERE ARE PEOPLE who cannot do any of what I have just explained, not even when it is proposed to them. Others, in contrast, carry it out with extreme ease. In meditation there is no objective ease or difficulty; everything depends on each person's resistances. Meditating is, fundamentally, sitting in silence, and sitting in silence is, fundamentally, observing the movements of the mind itself. Observing the mind is the path. Why? Because while observed, the mind does not think. Therefore, strengthening the observer is the way to end the tyranny of the mind, which is what marks the distance between the world and me.

In addition to observing the mind, there is another path: first to make oneself one with the breath and, then, to make oneself one with what is called koan. A koan is a sort of puzzle that Buddhist monks work with during their meditation, not with the aim of resolving it, but rather of dissolving themselves in it. I like to say that a koan is like a light along the path, thanks to which you know where you are and where you are headed. The fact is that whether by the path of emptying by pure observation, or by the narrowing path of working with the koan, one begins to arrive at union with oneself or, which is the same thing, to a betrothal to oneself.

Sitting and observing myself has enabled those sparks or intuitions that have allowed me to discover who I am much more than reflecting on my personality through the hackneyed path of analysis. Generally, when I sit and observe myself, not much time passes before I discover myself in another place. I have escaped from myself and I must return. At the end, I find myself outside again, generally fantasizing—I am very prone to fantasy—or speculating—I am also quite speculative—or worried about something that lies in wait for me in the future. Like almost all human beings, some things make me anxious. I meditate exactly as I live: with fears, with images, and with concepts.... There must be those who meditate and see mostly their past: the nostalgic ones; those who meditate and mostly see their partner: the romantic ones; and those who are victims of loads of stimuli without order: the scattered ones. No one sits to meditate with what they are not.

But it is not enough to sit in silence; one must observe what happens within. These are the rules of the game. The more you observe, the more you accept: it is a mathematical law, although familiarizing yourself with it can be more or less difficult. Sitting in silence, one obtains a mirror of life itself and, at the same time, a way to improve it. Observation, contemplation, is effective. Seeing something does not change it, but it changes us. Change is the best yardstick of a life's vitality. But change, and this is the most important thing, can be lived without drama.

29

IT IS HABITUAL that we prolong and enlarge our feelings to feel that we are alive, that things happen to us, and that our life is worthy of recounting. Of course, life is always a process of inquiry, and all of us are touched by it. But how many of our reactions are authentic reactions to life's questioning and how many, by contrast, are simple mental decisions that have taken questioning as an excuse, but have definitely left it far behind? In my opinion, we invent our moods to a great degree. We are responsible for our doing well or poorly. These artificial prolongations of emotions can be controlled and even aborted thanks to meditation, whose real purpose, as I understand it, is teaching one to live real life, not fictitious life.

Emotions? They are no more than the combination of a particular bodily sensation and particular thoughts. Mood? An emotion that is prolonged to a greater or lesser extent. Emotions and moods have their own function, but, if we acknowledge it, we are infinitely more powerful than they are. We do not have to endorse an emotion; we can face down a mood. We can create the mood that we desire. We can choose which role to play in the show, or even not to represent any character at all and to attend it as spectators. The show can continue and we can leave or it can finish and we can stay. The potential of our sovereignty is shocking.

30

FROM THIS PERSPECTIVE, I could define meditation as the spiritual method (and when I say "spiritual" I mean interior seeking) to unmask false illusions. We squander a good portion of our energy on illusory expectations: ghosts that disappear when we touch them. The illusory is always a product of the mind, which likes to distract us with tricks, to take us to a battlefield where there are no warriors, just smoke, and to bewilder us until we are incapable of reacting.

Those of us who dedicate ourselves to literature know very clearly that what springs from the mind is dead and that what springs from mysterious depths— which I, for lack of a better name, will call authentic—is alive. Those mysterious depths—the authentic I, not the small I—are the space that one attempts to visit during meditation. Those mysterious depths are like an empty stage. Precisely because it is empty, the things that enter it can be clearly distinguished. Meditating is moving the marionettes that one discovers to be illusory from that stage so that one is able to distinguish what bursts onto the scene. Among so many illusory marionettes, we do not regularly distinguish what is real. That is why the task of those who sit to meditate is, fundamentally, that of interior cleaning. The empty stage scares us; it gives us the impression that we will get bored in its desolation. But that emptiness is our most radical identity, it is nothing but pure capacity for reception.

31

I HAVE ARRIVED at these convictions by means of the only necessary question: Who am I? In attempting to respond, I realized that any attribute I give to that "I am"—any whatsoever—became, once seen properly, scandalously false. Because I could say, for example, "I am Pablo d'Ors," but the truth is that I would also be who I am if I substituted my name for another. In the same way, I could say, "I am a writer"; but then does that mean that I would not be who I am if in fact I did not write? Or "I'm a Christian," in which case, would I cease to be myself if I renounced my faith? Any attribute, even the most sublime, applied to the self is radically insufficient. The best definition of myself that I have come up with to this point is

"I am." Simply. Meditation is taking pleasure in and having a good time in this "I am."

Taking pleasure in simply being, if it comes through the appropriate channels, produces the best of possible intentions: alleviating the suffering of the world. Thanks to a process of internal expiation, one sits to meditate with their miseries to arrive at that "I am." And one sits with that "I am" to nourish compassion. But it is not simple to arrive at this point, given that we never finish purging.

All the world seems thirsty for something, and almost all of us run from here to there seeking to find it and satiate ourselves with it. In meditation, one recognizes that I am thirst, not just that I am thirsty; and one manages to end these crazy races or at least slow one's step. The water is in the thirst. It is necessary to enter the well itself. That deepening has nothing to do with the psychoanalytic technique of memory, nor with what is called composition of place, a method so beloved by the Ignatian tradition. What then?

32

ENTERING THE WELL itself means living through a long process of deception, and that is because everything, without exception, once acquired deceives us in one way or another. The work of art that we create deceives us, as intense as the process of creation or as beautiful as the final result might have been. The person we marry deceives us, because they ultimately do not turn out to be as we believed. The house that we have built deceives us, the vacations we planned, the child we had, none of these matches what we expected from them. Ultimately, we are deceived by the community that we live in, the God we believe in—who does not deal with our complaints—and even ourselves, who were so promising in our youth and who, when seen properly, have managed to accomplish so little. All these things, and so many others, deceive us because they do not match the idea that we had constructed. The problem resides, therefore, in the idea that we had made. Ideas are what deceive us. The discovery of disappointment is our primary teacher. Everything that disappoints me is my friend.

When you stop waiting for your partner to adjust to the standard you have made for them, you stop suffering because of it. When you stop waiting for the work that you are doing to adjust to the idea you have made of it, you stop suffering for that reason. Life passes us by in our effort to adjust it to our ideas and appetites. This happens even after a prolonged practice of meditation.

There is no need to give false hope to anyone; it is a feeble favor. It is necessary to get to the root of disappointment, which is none other than the pernicious fabrication of an illusion. The best help that we can give to someone is to accompany them in the process of disappointment that all the world suffers from in one way or another, and almost constantly. Helping someone is making them see that their efforts are misguided. Telling them, "You suffer because you bang your face against a wall. But you are bashing yourself against a wall because you are going where you should not be going." We do not need to crash against the majority of the walls we actually crash into. Those walls should not be there, we should not have constructed them.

33

WE ARE ALWAYS seeking solutions. We never learn that there is no solution. Our solutions are just patches, and that is how we go through life: from patch to patch. But, following proper logic, if there is no solution, there is no problem either. The problem and the solution are one and the same thing. That is why the best thing that we can do when we have a problem is to live it.

We fight duels that are not our own. We are castaways on seas that we should never have navigated. We live lives that are not ours, and that is why we die bewildered. The sad thing is not dying but doing so without having lived. Those who truly live are always willing to die; they know they have fulfilled their mission.

All of our ideas must die so that life can finally reign. And all means all, even the idea that we might have made of meditation. I, for example, began to meditate to improve my life; now I meditate simply to live it. If I consider it properly, I never live as much as when I sit to meditate. Because it is not the case that I live more when I meditate, but that I live more consciously, and consciousness—as I have already said—is nothing more than contact with oneself.

So, for me meditating is being with myself, while when I do not meditate I do not truly know where I am. Meditation does not fundamentally have to do with being happier or better—these come as an extra—but rather with being who you are. You are fine with what you are, that is what must be understood. Seeing that you are fine as you are, that is waking up.

Happiness is not the absence of unhappiness, but rather consciousness of it. As we cast light on our unhappiness, it loses some of its bite. Unhappiness is powerful and ruins us if we are unconscious of its cause and of its ramifications. Pain stops being so painful when you get used to it. I do not really know how I have arrived at such a discovery. Neither do I know how I have managed to be so perseverant in my daily practice of meditation, to which I have now been as faithful for about five years as I have been to writing for around a couple of decades.

In the beginning of my meditation practice, I worried a lot when I stopped meditating for a few days for some reason or another. With time, I noticed that I always returned to silence, that there was something in it that called to me. In meditation there is something that is difficult to eradicate once it has overpowered you. It is also difficult to know precisely what it is. It is as if we had been born to sit in silence; or as if we had been born to accompany breath itself, or to incessantly and slowly repeat a short prayer, in hope of someday managing to dissolve ourselves into it.

Silence is a calling, not a personal calling—as we Christians say who have felt that we have been chosen for a singular vocation—but a purely impersonal calling: the imperative of entering the unknown; the invitation to shed ourselves of everything insubstantial, in the belief that we will better find ourselves when stripped bare. Something or someone within us says: be quiet, listen. One can never be sure of having really heard that voice, but if we are in fact regularly quiet and listen, it is likely that we have heard it. If that were not the case, we would not find the strength to be silent and to listen.

34

THE PROMISE OF MEDITATION is the most mysterious of those I know, since it is not a promise of anything in particular: not of glory, not of power, not of pleasure. Perhaps it is a promise of unity, or a type of costly serenity, or of lucidity, or … words!

Silence creates a certain addiction. It has a first phase, a very first one, of enchantment. We tell ourselves, "What peace! How nice it is!" Or: "Finally, silence!" But a few minutes, or, in the best of cases, hours, are enough for that agreeable sensation to dissipate and for silence to display its more arid face: the desert.

That which one needs to recapitulate or tell oneself can normally be taken care of in a relatively short time. But what matters least about the experience of the desert is what we believe we need to tell ourselves; what matters most, on the other hand, is what silence has to tell us. Though the spectator who does not like a show gives up their seat and simply leaves, the true meditator remains in place even when the film projected in their interior is not at all pleasing. Then, most of all, they must remain.

We are so mysterious that the moment comes when even that which displeases us comes to entertain and amuse us. Without taking away its painful and frustrating character, that upsetting interior film can, from a certain point of view, also be considered fun. It turns out that confirming how we struggle to become our own selves can be fun. Fun? Well, yes. Truly seeing oneself really is fascinating and fun. At the end of the day, that is why we go to the cinema or read novels: so that they can tell us what we're like, to identify with the protagonist.

You are either conscious of your anger, of your nerves, and of your worries, or your nerves, your worries, or your anger control you. It is that simple: if you do not think about them, they will think for you and they will take you where you do not want to go. Ask yourself why you are angered, where your worry has sprung from, and how it is that you have become so nervous. You will realize that this inquiry turns out to be very curious and even fun. To be what one is has become the greatest challenge.

35

THE PRACTICE OF MEDITATION that I am referring to can be safely summarized as knowing how to be here and now. Not another place, not another time. This means that it is a practice of reunification, of reunion. We want to be with ourselves: our habitual unconsciousness avoids it, but our deepest conscious knows it.

It is difficult to descend to the depths where that wisdom lurks; most people that I know do not ever visit that area of their being. They are even ignorant that something like this exists. There are also those who make fun of those of us who speak in these terms. Those in this latter group are generally bookworms: they have only read, they have not lived; they believe that the world fits into a mental category.

Meditation in silence and stillness is the most direct and radical path toward the interior itself (it does not resort to imagination or to music, to give a couple examples, as other pathways do), and that requires a soldier's mettle and a very strong resolve. It is not exceptional that those who choose such a dry and difficult meditation have gone through many other spiritual disciplines of inner seeking; and neither is it unusual, insofar as I have been able to tell, that many leave their first sittings scared. Why? Because meditating in this way is something very physical and very sobering.

It is true that many intellectuals, without having sat to meditate even once, have felt attracted to silence, but such fascination, if it is not accompanied by practice, is worth very little. In silent meditation and stillness there is no adornment or flourish: a room that is neither too heated nor too cold is enough; a stool or cushion to sit on and a mat are enough; perhaps very mild incense, or even a small altar with a lit candle. Everything is in service of seclusion, all invites interiorization.

36

IT TAKES EXTRAORDINARY HUMILITY to sit down to meditate, which is to say, being willing to let go of ideals and ideas and to touch reality. Meditating helps one not to take oneself so seriously (a school of healthy self-relativization) and requires much patience, perseverance, and determination. The more patience, perseverance, and determination we acquire, the more we sit to meditate. That explains the importance of finding a group to regularly sit to meditate with.

Although one is alone and in silence before mystery, it is good to know that there are others—also silent and solitary—at one's side, before the same mystery. Those of us who meditate tend to be solitary birds. There will be other birds in the flock, but each one will follow their own rhythm. In fact, among the Friends of the Desert, which is the name of the group I occasionally sit with to meditate, we are very careful to avoid comparison between each other, which is what always destroys any human grouping. As I see it, these friends I come together with are more a congregation of solitary practitioners than a community. But we are a congregation that stimulates the practice itself, not just because of the energy that the meditators generate, but also because, stimulated by the example of others, one tends to be more disciplined with oneself. Having a group of companions to get together to meditate with is a great treasure. I also highly recommend having a teacher or partner with whom to share your doubts and fears as you travel the path.

37

YOU CAN HOLD important titles or none at all, be lettered or illiterate, have had thousands of experiences or very few, have come on long journeys or from a small and unknown town—none of these things is a condition to be able to meditate, and none at all is an impediment. It does not matter what your past has been. The baggage that you carry with you does not count, but rather you do, just you, all the rest is of no concern and can even get in your way.

I feel the highest level of respect toward the man I consider my teacher, and not just because of the luminous words he has always given me, but because of his incredible sense of humor. Elmar Salmann, that is his name, laughs at everything, but fundamentally at himself. Accustomed as we are to facing people infinitely preoccupied with their image and reputation, it is unheard of to find ourselves before someone who is indifferent to what you think or stop thinking about them. This amazes because of its rarity, but most of all because of the sovereignty that it displays. It is attractive because it is what we are all called to: the forgetting of oneself.

Among all the things that place themselves between us and reality, among all those things that impede our living because they act like deforming filters, the hardest to eradicate is that which is known in Zen Buddhism as the ego. Salmann, who as well as being a Benedictine monk is a true sage, as are the three Zen teachers with whom I have been in contact to varying degrees, has fought his ego in a battle to the death. Seeing this, realizing how they have tamed it without losing their character is instructive. All of them move resolutely and say simply what they have in their hearts and heads, without seeming to worry about the repercussions or the impressions they could provoke. The words they speak are the words they speak. They have no ulterior motive. One does not have to ponder what they say, one does not have to untangle or interpret it. You simply have to take it as is, if you wish; or toss it aside if they are not the opportune words for you at that moment.

There should be no deification in all that I write about these teachers, and in particular about the one I consider my own. Being as he is, without any sort of strategy, Salmann makes it clear that I am not yet who I truly am, but rather still someone too cunning and unnecessarily complex. Nonetheless, I have never left a conversation with him feeling ashamed of myself. More accurately I would say that I leave rejuvenated. I would say that the simple act of placing oneself before an authentic person is rejuvenating.

Our discussions or interviews have never happened in ethical or moral terms—as is quite typical in Catholicism—but rather purely phenomenological, so to speak: we note facts and, at most, he offers me a possible hermeneutics of them: something like clues to work through or a horizon to approach. Salmann has always offered friends for the journey (authors and books in whose wake to follow for their intuitions and to drink from their spring); a simple but coherent map with which to orient myself in this slippery and unexplored territory that is the soul; and, finally, something like an opening to an enormous panorama thanks to which one can breathe again and get excited before the fullness of what they have before them. When I fall, my teacher does not pick me up, but elegantly shows me that it is much better to stand up. He also teaches me to laugh at my resistances. In his teachings, there is a perfect combination of strictness and indulgence, humor and gravity.

38

WHEN ONE SEEKS oneself enough, what one ends up finding is the world. In truth, I never change, or I change very little, but the way in which I face myself changes, and that is fundamental. As in art, as in life, point of view in meditation is not mere nuance, but the key to the vault or the cornerstone.

To observe oneself well, one's gaze must be oblique or lateral, never direct. We tend to escape from ourselves when we look at ourselves directly. Obliquely, by contrast, as if wanting to trick the self that we gaze at, that substantial self stays longer and we can take heed of it, being finally conscious of what we observe. This is how I have come to understand that what we truly seek is the seeker, and that in well-undertaken meditation everything fades or melts away except exactly that which is observed. That, the observer, the witness, is what is permanent.

When thoughts and feelings, images and ideas leave, what is it that remains? What you seek remains, and it is good to look at what you seek obliquely. The oblique gaze should be attentive but not fixed. It does not consist of looking penetratingly, attempting to dig deeper or untangle who knows what, but rather to look lovingly, without any aim, like one who awaits a revelation without any hurry. In Zen, it is said that a monk without illumination is worthless; but also that the path is the goal. What is important is the waiting, which, like the drop of water that splashes on a rock, bores into us little by little.

39

ALMOST ALL OF THE FRUITS of meditation are perceived outside of meditation. Some of those fruits are, for example, a greater acceptance of life as it is, a greater acceptance of one's limitations and of one's aches and pains, a greater benevolence toward one's fellows, a more careful attention to the needs of others, a greater appreciation of animals and nature, a more global and less analytical vision of the world, and a growing openness to diversity, humility, self-confidence, and serenity. The list could go on.

Through the constant practice of meditation, it is proven that if you have plowed your consciousness into consciousness and have abandoned yourself well, everything will grow splendidly. Living is preparing oneself for life. All efforts invested in oneself bears fruit sooner or later. Of course, the fruits tend to be slow to be harvested, but they are harvested, they are certainly harvested: like the artists who, after long years of training, give light—gracefully, as if nothing—to a masterpiece. It has not been gracefully, it has not been as if nothing. The trunk had roots; the fruit was ripe.

40

THE GAZE INTO that is practiced during silent meditation and in stillness tends gradually to be used outside only the time devoted to it, so that one learns to be in the world with a receptive, generous, respectful, non-violent attitude. It is also a good practice to observe all these changes in one's character or temperament. These transformations of temperament or behavior can be summarized in just one shift: the dissolution of the small I. The false identities to which we tend to succumb I call the ego or the small I. Those mirages that make us run after nothing gradually keep shrinking the more one meditates. It is obvious that this small I writhes and resists; it is obvious that our false I plays tricks on the real I so that things remain as they are; and it is obvious, finally, that there are frequently steps backwards. Because the ego always reappears, although transformed, since no one can live without it.

One of the first threats to this whole process of interior purification rests in the belief—sustained by those who have not meditated or have done so very little—that all of this preoccupation about the self does not serve to help others. In this respect, I will say something I have frequently affirmed and that tends to surprise others: the ideology of altruism has sneaked into our Western minds, be it by the pathway of Christianity or be it by that of atheist humanism. In Zen Buddhism, by contrast, it appears to be very clear that the best way to help others is by being oneself and that it is difficult—if not impossible—to know what is best for another, since to do so one would have to be the other and be in their circumstances. Said with greater conviction: all help to any you is purely superficial until I discover that I am you, that you are me, and that we are all one. Consequently, the most appropriate thing appears to be letting you be what you are. Believing that one can help is almost always a presumption. Zen teaches us to leave others in peace because little of what happens to them is truly our business. Almost all our problems begin by getting involved where we are not invited.

41

IT IS EVIDENT that for a Westerner all of this can sound very convenient and even unreal. But there is nothing further from the truth: to remain where one belongs is not an easy task; to go only where we are really called is more complicated than it seems at first glance. If we are sincere, we will recognize that there are few who have truly helped us, though there are many who have attempted (or say they have attempted). In Zen, one attempts nothing: things are done or not done, but not attempted. And in Zen—as in Taoism—there is a singular preference for not doing, convinced that a good part of the things in this world would work better without human intervention, which tends to distort the world's natural rhythm or to create side effects of incalculable proportions.

The funny thing—not to call it pathetic—is that we are in the thick of life and expect to leave it unscathed. Such presumption of being able to splash around in the mud without getting muddy is certainly illusory. The more we attempt to avoid life's beatings, the more life insists we realize what it is or can become.

Given that we are in life, let us live it! That seems like the most sensible option. If we must learn to swim, it is better for us to throw ourselves into the water than to spend too much time thinking about it on the edge. This is exactly our problem in life: the hesitations, the fears, the systematic doubts, the fear of living. It is always smarter to throw oneself into the adventure. Meditation unmasks our defense mechanisms, it projects them on a large scale onto the screen of our consciousness, it shows us all that we have lost because of the safeguards encouraged by social conventions and pressures of every type.

42

LIKE ANY OTHER serious method of inner analysis, silent meditation in stillness emphasizes the fallacy of attributing to the other what corresponds to ourselves. In reality, wanting something intensely enough is sufficient to acquire it. It sounds utopian, but there is nothing more indestructible as a human being who is convinced. No obstacle is insurmountable when there is true faith. Meditation strengthens that faith and, with an ardent gaze, melts the obstacles that one finds on the path as if they were blocks of ice unable to hold up against a passion's fire.

One should meditate open to surrendering everything, like a soldier who goes to war entirely alone. Because, at the moment of truth, that is what we are: alone. At the end of a path we are always alone, and sometimes in the middle of that path too. Rarely, on the other hand, at its beginning. Neither your partner nor your family nor your friends, not even God, seems to come to our help at decisive moments. Everyone is very occupied with their things, and we should be with ours. It is not about egoism or about indifference, but rather about simple responsibility: one must answer for oneself. In the court of our conscience, we have to give account of what we have received and of what we are going to leave in the world before dying and departing it.

43

I, OF COURSE, do not really know what life is, but I have determined to live it. I do not want to lose out on any of the life that has been given to me. I do not just oppose missing out on big experiences, but also—and most of all—the smallest ones. I want to learn as much as I can, I want to taste the flavor of what is offered me. I am not willing to clip my wings or for anyone else to clip them for me. I am over forty years old and I still think about flying through as many skies as I am presented with, sailing as many seas as I have the opportunity of reaching, and breeding in any nest that welcomes me. I want to have children, plant trees, and write books. I want to scale mountains and dive in the oceans. To smell the flowers, love women, play with children, and pet animals. I am open to the rain's getting me wet and the breeze tickling me, to being cold in the winter and hot in the summer. I have learned that it is good to reach out a hand to the elderly, to look into the eyes of the dying, to listen to music, and to read stories. I opt to converse with my fellows, recite prayers, and celebrate rituals. I will get up in the morning and lie down at night, I will sit beneath the sun's rays, I will admire the stars, I will gaze at the moon and allow myself to be gazed upon by her. I want to build houses and leave for foreign lands, speak languages, traverse deserts, chase trails, and bite into fruits. Make friends. Bury the dead. Cradle newborn babies. I want to know as many teachers as can teach me and to be a teacher myself. I want to work in schools and hospitals, in universities, and in workshops. I want to lose myself in forests, to run along beaches, and to see the horizon from the cliffs. In meditation, I hear that I should not deprive myself of anything, given that everything is good. Life is a splendid journey, and to live it there is only one thing that must be dealt with: fear.

Of all the dilemmas that I know, the biggest is life itself. Who can solve it? Life is everything but safe, despite our absurd attempts to make it so. One lives or one dies, and those who choose the first option must accept the risk. We are at the table, before the game board, everything has been conjured up so that we take the dice cup, shake it, and throw the dice. It saddens me to think that there are many who have that dice cup in their hands and even manage to shake it, but without allowing those playful, noisy dice to shoot out and roll across the board. And it saddens me that there are many who spend life with their gaze fixed on that board but without ever deciding to play, many who doubt whether they should or should not sit at the banquet table open to them; many who go to the river and do not swim, or to the mountain without climbing it, or to life without living it, or to humanity without loving it. I have the impression that meditation has only been invented to eradicate fear. Or at least to face and accept it, to put a stop to the right things so that it does not end in panic.

One can live without fighting against life. Why go against life if one can go along with it? Why consider life as an act of combat instead of as an act of love? A year of persistent meditation—or even half a year—is enough to realize that one can live another way. Meditation cracks the structure of our personality until, from so much meditating, the crack widens and the old personality breaks and, like a flower, a new one begins to be born. Meditating is assisting this fascinating and tremendous process of death and rebirth.

44

OF COURSE, IT IS POSSIBLE to live without being born twice, but it is not worth it. It is better to be reborn, and not just twice, but many times: all that we are capable of. How many lives fit into a life? This is important because growth does not have the same magic as beginnings. There is something unique in every genesis: a strength, an impulse. The most decisive thing about any activity—including sitting meditation—is the beginning: the initial disposition, the energy that is expended, the first breath or enthusiasm. Every time we suffer some serious setback in life, we are called to be reborn from our ashes, to reinvent ourselves.

Imagine for a moment the thing you most desire and also imagine that you do not get it. Well, you can be happy without getting it: this is what meditation gives us. Frustration can be worked out creatively, without resignation. All of us desire things but can know full well that our human fulfillment does not depend on the attainment of those things. In reality, I am understanding that what has to happen always happens. What happens is always the best thing that could have happened. Transformation is much wiser than our ideas or plans. Thinking the opposite is an error of perspective and the ultimate cause of our suffering and of our unhappiness. We suffer only because we think that things should be another way. Inasmuch as we abandon that presumption, we stop suffering. Inasmuch as we stop imposing our schemes on reality, reality stops seeming adverse or favorable to us and begins to manifest itself as it is, without the standard of valuation that impedes our accessing reality itself. That is why the path of meditation is that of unattachment, that of the breakdown of mental schemes or preconceptions. Meditation is an undressing that ultimately proves that one is much better naked.

We are so lamentably devoted to our points of view that if we could see ourselves with true objectivity we would feel shame and even compassion for ourselves. The world has grave problems to resolve and we human beings are generally engaged with minuscule problems that reveal our shortsightedness and our incorrigible stinginess. The main fruit of meditation is that it makes us magnanimous, which is to say, it widens our soul: soon more colors, more people, more shapes and figures begin to fit inside. In reality, the greater a human being's capacity for hosting or receiving, the more noble they are. The emptier we are of ourselves, the more will fit inside of us. The emptiness of self, the forgetfulness of self, is in direct proportion to one's love for others. Christ and Buddha are, in this sense, the most illustrious examples I know.

45

ATTACHMENT IS COMPLETELY INDEPENDENT of the thing that is attached to. We can feel attachment toward our mother, but also toward a simple notebook (and this second attachment can be even more visceral than the first!). Attachment has to do with the ideological apparatus that encloses what we have and, most of all, our manner of having or not having. Meditation is a way to purge attachments; that is why it is not pleasant in the first instance. Only by crossing that purgative pathway does meditation become an illuminative pathway; but the path is worth the pain of walking it even when one does not reach a grand enlightenment. Simple purgation—and it is not simple—is worthwhile.

Ultimately it is the same if one advances much or little, the important thing is to always advance, to persevere, to take a step each day. Satisfaction is not obtained at the goal, but on the path itself. A human being is a pilgrim, a homo viator.

In meditation I have learned—I am learning—that nothing is stronger than I am if I do not attach myself to it. Of course, things touch me, viruses infect me, the currents pull me, or temptations tempt me. Of course, I get hungry if I do not eat, thirsty if I do not drink, tired if I do not sleep; of course I am sensitive to a lover's caress, to a beggar's outstretched hand, to the lament of a sick man, or the cry of a baby. But once touched or infected, tempted or pulled, once in love or heartbroken it is I who decides—as my own master—how to live out that caress or that blow, that cry or that moan, how to react to that current, or respond to that demand. As long as I can say "I," I am the master of myself. I am also a creature, after all, but I have a consciousness that, without shedding my condition as a creature, elevates me to a superior status.

46

WE WILL NOT IRREDEEMABLY lose ourselves if we frequent our consciousness and travel through its inner territory. Within us there is a redoubt where we can feel secure: a hermitage, a hideout to shelter us because it has been prepared to that end. The deeper one goes into it, the more one discovers how spacious and well equipped it is. In truth, it lacks nothing. One can live there very well.

At the beginning, because of its darkness, we need a lantern to guide us through this refuge; but then our eyes grow accustomed to the darkness and, finally, we do not even understand how we could have once needed an artificial light to see. Everything is so clear! Everything is so luminous!

In the country of consciousness itself there are many dwellings. It is like a castle with walls, turrets, and drawbridges. It is like an island or, more accurately, an archipelago. There you have a greater dominion than you could ever imagine in any kingdom. You give an order and it is obeyed; your desires are fulfilled before you have formed them. It is a place that is full and empty at the same time. In it you are alone, but you do not feel alone. This territory is a world, your world, the mirror of another world, the same world but concentrated, dilated, expanded: your home.

This big, beautiful house is what we are. I am that, you are that; whether we know it or not, we are the lords of an entire kingdom. The expanse of our domains is formidable and the unconsciousness we hold them with is sad.

Meditation strengthens the necessary distrust in the external world and the indispensable trust in our true world, which we tend not to know. If we meditate, our features soften and our expression is transfigured. We continue here, on this earth, but it is as if we no longer belong here. We inhabit another country, seldom frequented, and we traverse battlefields without being injured. It is not that the arrows do not hit us or that the bullets do not sink into our flesh; but neither do those bullets knock us over nor those arrows make us bleed. We leave those battlefields riddled with bullets, but alive: walking and smiling because we have not succumbed, and we have demonstrated our eternity. We meditate to be stronger than death.

No one really knows what the human being's consciousness is, because no one has traveled all of its domains. Some have gone very far in their explorations; many have remained at the doorway; most do not know that such a territory exists. Like a microcosm, everything from outside is there too: the universe, galaxies, trees, springs.... Everything without exception has its place there: the rivers and mountains, trails and precipices, childhood games, machines.... In that space you can lose yourself without worry. Take a step and you are far away, a thousand and you remain near. It is the garden of astonishment and wonder.

47

WITHIN US THERE is a witness. Whether we acknowledge it or not, that witness is always there. Meditating is letting the witness in, reviving it. If we look at it, it looks at us. Living with the inner witness is much more intelligent than ignoring it. It is in this sense that it can be said that we seek the seeker. There is an (authentic) I who looks at the other (false) I. Living adequately, meditating, assumes remaining in that gaze without presumptions. One who meditates sooner or later finds that witness: at first, it fades and looks blurry, but little by little its contours become sharper, without ever reaching the moment when we have trapped and can domesticate it. One must summon that witness in meditation, but most of all one must wait for it. It will appear amidst the mists sometimes, then it will hide again.

Later, quite a bit later, what we can call the witness of the witness will begin to appear during meditation. It is there, in that witness of the witness, where one must remain for as long as possible. Someone—who is I—looks at me (at the apparent I), and someone—perhaps God—looks at the I that I look at. That witness of the witness is only accessed in very deep meditation and there are no words to describe it. When we try to put it into words, it stops being there.

Despite how unknown it is, the inner territory can be said to be magnetic: as little as we know it, the truth is that it beckons us and irresistibly attracts us. As I see it and feel it, it is the call of the homeland, the call of identity. "I am your land," the inner territory tells us. "Come." Then we embark on the path toward that goal: a torturous path, full of stones and undergrowth. We clear the terrain, making it ever easier to travel, until before long, when we had happily promised it to ourselves, the goal disappears, the path blurs and we are devastated again, on foreign land.

You are the promised land, that is what is learned in meditation. You cannot despair, given that the treasure is in you and you carry it always with you; at any moment you can take refuge in it if you wish. You have a fortress in your heart, and it is unassailable.

From this perspective, living is transforming oneself into what one is. The more you enter the inner territory, the more naked you are. First you remove things, then you leave people behind; first you take off your clothes, then your skin; little by little you start pulling apart your bones, so that your skeleton—it is worth the metaphor—is ever more elemental. When you have taken it all off, you finally leave behind your skull. When you no longer have nor are anything, you are finally free. You are the inner territory itself: you are not just in your homeland, you are your homeland.

This journey can be done in life: the great mystics have done it, are doing it. They have emptied so much of themselves that they are almost transparent. "You should empty yourself of everything that is not you": that is the invitation that one permanently hears when one meditates. God can only enter what is empty and pure. That is why Jesus Christ entered the Virgin Mary's womb. We are called, or at least this is how I see it, to this fecund spiritual virginity.

48

THE QUESTION OF SPIRITUAL VIRGINITY, of the heart's purity, or of primordial innocence is the one that truly counts; all the others are false questions, false problems.

We live lives that are not ours; we respond to inquiries that no one has posed; we complain of illnesses from which we do not suffer; we aspire to foreign ideals and dream the dreams of others. This is not an exaggeration, it is so: almost all of our projects for happiness are unrealistic. The ideas we say we cling to are not ours; our aspirations are those of our parents, and we even fall in love with people whom we do not truly like. What has happened for us to succumb to such fraud? I chase something that, at my core, I do not desire. I struggle for something that I am indifferent to. I have a house interchangeable with my neighbor's. I take a trip and see nothing. I go on vacation and I do not rest. I read a book and I do not understand. I hear a phrase and I am incapable of repeating it. How is it possible that I am not moved before a person in need, that I do not respond when I am asked something, that I always look elsewhere and that I do not know where I actually am?

Faced with this absurd situation, I am going to stop, I am going to think, to breathe, and to be born, if it is possible, for a second time. I am unwilling not to dance when the flute plays or not to eat when I am offered a delicacy. I will not store up for tomorrow when there are those who do not have today. Neither am I willing to believe myself to be the navel of the world, nor to assume that what is mine is best, nor to martyr myself with diminutive problems or imaginary pains. It is regrettable to have reached this point of unconsciousness, of stupidity, of insensitivity, this extreme of avarice, arrogance, and laziness…. The world is not a cake that I have to eat. The other is not an object for me to use. The Earth is not a planet made for me to exploit. I am not a predatory monster. That is why I have decided to stand up and open my eyes. I have decided to eat and drink in moderation, to sleep as necessary, to write only what contributes toward improving those who read me, to abstain from greed, and never compare myself to my fellows. I have also decided to water my plants and care for an animal. I will visit the sick, I will converse with the lonely, and I will not let much time go by before playing with a child. In the same manner I have also decided to recite my prayers each day, to bow several times before the things I consider sacred, to celebrate the Eucharist, to listen to the Word, to break the bread and share the wine, to give peace, to sing in unison. And to go for walks, which I find essential. And to light the fire, which is also essential. And to shop without hurry, to greet my neighbors even when I do not like seeing their faces, to subscribe to a newspaper, to regularly call my friends and siblings on the phone. And to take excursions, swim in the sea at least once a year, and to only read good books, or reread those that I have liked.

Meditation—or should I simply say maturity?—has taught me to appreciate the ordinary, the elemental. I will live for those things according to an ethics of attention and care. And this is how I will arrive at a happy old age, when I will contemplate, humble and proud at the same time, the small but grand orchard that I have cultivated. Life as cult, culture, and cultivation.

49

THESE ARE MY DECISIONS, but while trying to give them life it is difficult for me to accept that I am not going to achieve even one of them simply by sitting to meditate.

That just by meditating I am not going to get absolutely anything. Because meditating is infinitely more sterile (although also infinitely more fecund) than everything that one can imagine. What I have written in these pages is a pale reflection of my experience; my words remain too close or too far away.... Talking or writing about silent meditation is, in truth, a contradiction, a paradox. That is precisely why none of this will serve anyone very much. Further still: the most advisable thing to do would be to quit reading already and start meditating. Because any meditation, even the shortest one, even the most scattered, is good for the soul. Sitting to meditate in silence is almost always the best thing that one can do.

In my case, I began to do meditation because I noticed that I lived with so imperious a desire that it took away my peace: that of triumphing as a writer. So then, not too many years ago, I noticed perfectly that this desire could be fulfilled or not; but neither was it hidden from me that—no matter how great my triumph—I would always consider it insufficient and that, consequently, my happiness should not depend on such an untrustworthy expectation. Harassed by the thirst for recognition and, still more, for posterity, my inner teacher warned me that that was a race without a finishing line. To the degree that I meditated, my initial motivation faded, and other, new ones appeared: to be better, to live more intensely, to enjoy nature more, to feel one with others.... It would be false to suggest that my eagerness for literary glory has fully disappeared, and naive to think that this search—so often a motor—could be turned entirely off; but I no longer go out of my way because of it or let my well-being depend on its achievement. I have the premonition—almost the conviction—that in letters, as in everything else, I will triumph to the degree that corresponds to my merits. Do not ask me why.

This means I have lost the utilitarianism with which I began to meditate. Each time I center myself more on the practice itself, and less on the neighboring assumptions that it tends to be adorned with so that it does not look so dry. Because sobriety has its charm—no one is going to deny it—but it is costly to find it. Walking along a steppe is boring, it is much more entertaining to do so through a forest or in the mountains.

My goal is not to be important today, nor even to be someone. An aspiration of this type is senseless: I am already someone, I am already important.... When I meditate just because, and for no other reason, I will begin to do true meditation. In the meantime, I will be approaching and distancing myself, flirting with things, bathing myself, and putting away my clothes. I am just missing a little bit more silence to overcome all of this, a little bit more meditation. If I have written these pages it is precisely to expand my faith in silence, which is why the most sensible thing is for me to now leave behind my words and throw myself, trusting, into that dark and luminous ocean that is silence.

DECEMBER 2010

MADRID, SPAIN

GUIDE TO
BIOGRAPHY OF SILENCE

ABOUT THE AUTHOR

PABLO d'ORS is a Spanish priest and writer. He was born in Madrid in 1963 and educated in New York, Vienna, Prague, and Rome. He was ordained in 1991 and he received a doctorate in theology in 1996. In 2014, he founded the Amigos del Desierto foundation with the aim of promoting the practice of meditation. In the same year, Pope Francis made him a consultant of the Pontifical Council for Culture. d'Ors debuted as a writer in 2000 with *El estreno,* a critically acclaimed collection of short stories. His essay *Biografía del silencio* was a publishing phenomenon in Spain, selling 130,000 copies in just a few years. Pablo d'Ors has gone on to publish almost a dozen fiction and non-fiction titles, which have been translated into French, German, Italian, Portuguese, and other languages. This is his first English translation.

DAVID SHOOK is a poet and translator in Los Angeles. He has translated over fifteen books from Spanish and Isthmus Zapotec, as well as shorter translations and cotranslations from nineteen languages.

PARALLAX PRESS, a nonprofit publisher founded by Zen Master Thich Nhat Hanh, publishes books and media on the art of mindful living and Engaged Buddhism. We are committed to offering teachings that help transform suffering and injustice. Our aspiration is to contribute to collective insight and awakening, bringing about a more joyful, healthy, and compassionate society.

For a copy of the catalog, please contact:

PARALLAX PRESS
P.O. BOX 7355
BERKELEY, CA 94707
PARALLAX.ORG